NUMBER AND OPERATIONS – TASK & DRILL SHEETS
Principles & Standards of Math Series

Written by Nat Reed

GRADES 6 – 8

Classroom Complete Press
P.O. Box 19729
San Diego, CA 92159
Tel: 1-800-663-3609 | Fax: 1-800-663-3608
Email: service@classroomcompletepress.com

www.classroomcompletepress.com

ISBN-13: 978-1-55319-544-3

© 2011

Process Standards Rubric

Number and Operations – Task & Drill Sheets

Number and Operations – Task Sheets

Exercise columns: 1, 2, 3, 4, 5, 6, 7, 8, 9, 10, 11, 12, 13, 14, 15, Drill Sheet 1, Drill Sheet 2, Review A, Review B, Review C

Expectations
Instructional programs from pre-kindergarten through grade 12 should enable all students to:

GOAL 1: Problem Solving
- build new mathematical knowledge through problem solving;
- solve problems that arise in mathematics and in other contexts;
- apply and adapt a variety of appropriate strategies to solve problems;
- monitor and reflect on the process of mathematical problem solving.

GOAL 2: Reasoning & Proof
- recognize reasoning and proof as fundamental aspects of mathematics;
- make and investigate mathematical conjectures;
- develop and evaluate mathematical arguments and proofs;
- select and use various types of reasoning and methods of proof.

GOAL 3: Communication
- organize and consolidate their mathematical thinking through communication;
- communicate their mathematical thinking coherently and clearly to peers, teachers, and others;
- analyze and evaluate the mathematical thinking and strategies of others;
- use the language of mathematics to express mathematical ideas precisely.

GOAL 4: Connections
- recognize and use connections among mathematical ideas;
- understand how mathematical ideas interconnect and build on one another to produce a coherent whole;
- recognize and apply mathematics in contexts outside of mathematics.

GOAL 5: Representation
- create and use representations to organize, record, and communicate mathematical ideas;
- select, apply, and translate among mathematical representations to solve problems;
- use representations to model and interpret physical, social, and mathematical phenomena.

Number and Operations – Task & Drill Sheets CC3312

Process Standards Rubric

Number and Operations – Task & Drill Sheets

Number and Operations – Drill Sheets

Expectations

Instructional programs from pre-kindergarten through grade 12 should enable all students to:

GOAL 1: Problem Solving
- build new mathematical knowledge through problem solving;
- solve problems that arise in mathematics and in other contexts;
- apply and adapt a variety of appropriate strategies to solve problems;
- monitor and reflect on the process of mathematical problem solving.

GOAL 2: Reasoning & Proof
- recognize reasoning and proof as fundamental aspects of mathematics;
- make and investigate mathematical conjectures;
- develop and evaluate mathematical arguments and proofs;
- select and use various types of reasoning and methods of proof.

GOAL 3: Communication
- organize and consolidate their mathematical thinking through communication;
- communicate their mathematical thinking coherently and clearly to peers, teachers, and others;
- analyze and evaluate the mathematical thinking and strategies of others;
- use the language of mathematics to express mathematical ideas precisely.

GOAL 4: Connections
- recognize and use connections among mathematical ideas;
- understand how mathematical ideas interconnect and build on one another to produce a coherent whole;
- recognize and apply mathematics in contexts outside of mathematics.

GOAL 5: Representation
- create and use representations to organize, record, and communicate mathematical ideas;
- select, apply, and translate among mathematical representations to solve problems;
- use representations to model and interpret physical, social, and mathematical phenomena.

Drills

Drill Sheet	Goal 1: Problem Solving	Goal 2: Reasoning & Proof	Goal 3: Communication	Goal 4: Connections	Goal 5: Representation
Warm-up 1	✓	✓ ✓	✓ ✓	✓	✓ ✓ ✓
Timed Drill 1	✓ ✓	✓ ✓	✓ ✓	✓	✓ ✓
Timed Drill 2	✓ ✓	✓	✓ ✓	✓	✓ ✓
Warm-up 2	✓ ✓	✓	✓		✓ ✓ ✓
Timed Drill 3	✓ ✓	✓ ✓			✓ ✓
Timed Drill 4	✓	✓			✓ ✓ ✓
Warm-up 3	✓ ✓	✓	✓ ✓		✓ ✓
Timed Drill 5	✓				✓ ✓ ✓
Timed Drill 6	✓ ✓	✓	✓ ✓	✓	✓ ✓
Warm-up 4	✓ ✓	✓	✓		✓ ✓
Timed Drill 7	✓ ✓	✓	✓	✓ ✓	✓ ✓ ✓
Timed Drill 8	✓	✓ ✓	✓	✓ ✓	✓ ✓
Warm-up 5	✓	✓ ✓		✓ ✓	✓ ✓ ✓
Timed Drill 9	✓	✓		✓ ✓	✓ ✓
Warm-up 6	✓ ✓	✓ ✓ ✓	✓	✓	✓ ✓ ✓
Timed Drill 10	✓	✓		✓ ✓	✓ ✓
Timed Drill 11	✓	✓		✓ ✓	✓ ✓ ✓
Review A	✓	✓		✓ ✓	✓ ✓ ✓
Review B	✓	✓ ✓		✓ ✓	✓ ✓ ✓
Review C	✓	✓ ✓		✓ ✓	✓ ✓ ✓

Contents

✔ **6 BONUS** Activity Pages! **Additional worksheets for your students**

FREE!

- Go to our website: **www.classroomcompletepress.com/bonus**
- Enter item CC3112
- Enter pass code CC3112D for Activity Pages.

Contents

✔ **6 BONUS** Activity Pages! **Additional worksheets for your students**

• Go to our website: **www.classroomcompletepress.com/bonus**
• Enter item CC3212
• Enter pass code CC3212D for Activity Pages.

FREE!

NCTM Content Standards Assessment Rubric

Number and Operations – Task & Drill Sheets

Student's Name: _____ Assignment: _____ Level: _____

	Level 1	Level 2	Level 3	Level 4
Understanding Numbers, Ways of Representing Numbers, Relationships Among Number Systems	• Demonstrates a limited understanding of numbers, ways of representing numbers and relationships among number systems	• Demonstrates a basic understanding of numbers, ways of representing numbers and relationships among number systems	• Demonstrates a good understanding of numbers, ways of representing numbers and relationships among number systems	• Demonstrates a thorough understanding of numbers, ways of representing numbers and relationships among number systems
Understanding Meanings of Operations and How They Relate to One Another	• Demonstrates a limited understanding of the meanings of operations and how they relate to one another	• Demonstrates a basic understanding of the meanings of operations and how they relate to one another	• Demonstrates a good understanding of the meanings of operations and how they relate to one another	• Demonstrates a thorough understanding of the meanings of operations and how they relate to one another
Computing and Making Estimates	• Demonstrates limited ability in computing and making estimates	• Demonstrates some ability in computing and making estimates	• Demonstrates satisfactory ability in computing and making estimates	• Demonstrates strong ability in computing and making estimates

STRENGTHS:

WEAKNESSES:

NEXT STEPS:

Teacher Guide

Our resource has been created for ease of use by both TEACHERS and STUDENTS alike.

Introduction

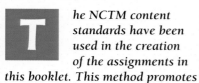

The NCTM content standards have been used in the creation of the assignments in this booklet. This method promotes the idea that it is beneficial to learn through practical, applicable, real-world examples. Many of the task and drill sheets are organized around a central problem taken from real-life experiences of the students. The pages of this booklet contain a variety in terms of levels of difficulty and content so as to provide students with a variety of different opportunities. Included are problems using multiplication and division, place value, fractions, percent and decimals. Visual models are included to assist visual learners. Teachers may also choose to use mathematics manipulatives along with the exercises included in this book to help address the needs of kinesthetic learners.

How Is Our Resource Organized?

STUDENT HANDOUTS

Reproducible **task sheets** and **drill sheets** make up the majority of our resource.

The **task sheets** contain challenging problem-solving tasks in drill form, many centered around 'real-world' ideas or problems, which push the boundaries of critical thought and demonstrate to students why mathematics is important and applicable in the real world. It is not expected that all activities will be used, but are offered for variety and flexibility in teaching and assessment. Many of the drill sheet problems offer space for reflection, and opportunity for the appropriate use of technology, as encouraged by the NCTM's *Principles & Standards for School Mathematics*.

The **drill sheets** contain 11 Timed Drill Sheets and 6 Warm-Up Drill Sheets, featuring real-life problem-solving opportunities. The drill sheets are provided to help students with their procedural proficiency skills, as emphasized by the *NCTM's Curriculum Focal Points*.

The **NCTM Content Standards Assessment Rubric** (*page 6*) is a useful tool for evaluating students' work in many of the activities in our resource. The **Reviews** (*pages 26-28 and 46-48*) are divided by grade and can be used for a follow-up review or assessment at the completion of the unit.

PICTURE CUES

Our resource contains three main types of pages, each with a different purpose and use. A **Picture Cue** at the top of each page shows, at a glance, what the page is for.

 Teacher Guide

* Information and tools for the teacher

 Student Handout

* Reproducible drill sheets

 Easy Marking™ Answer Key

* Answers for student activities

 Timed Drill Stopwatch

* Write the amount of time for students to complete the timed drill sheet in the stopwatch. Recommended times are given on the contents page.

EASY MARKING™ ANSWER KEY

Marking students' worksheets is fast and easy with our **Answer Key**. Answers are listed in columns – just line up the column with its corresponding worksheet, as shown, and see how every question matches up with its answer!

Every question matches up with its answer!

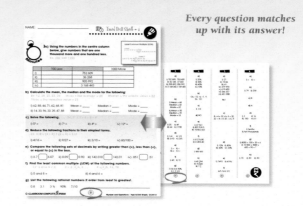

Principles & Standards

Principles & Standards for School Mathematics outlines the essential components of an effective school mathematics program.

The NCTM's Principles & Standards for School Mathematics

The **Principles** are the fundamentals to an effective mathematics education. The **Standards** are descriptions of what mathematics instruction should enable students to learn. Together the **Principles and Standards** offer a comprehensive and coherent set of learning goals, serving as a resource to teachers and a framework for curriculum. Our resource offers exercises written to the NCTM Process and **Content Standards** and is inspired by the **Principles** outlined below.

Six Principles for School Mathematics

Equity

Curriculum

Teaching

Learning

Assessment

Technology

EQUITY: All students can learn mathematics when they have access to high-quality instruction, including reasonable and appropriate accommodation and appropriately challenging content.

CURRICULUM: The curriculum must be coherent, focused, and well articulated across the grades, with ideas linked to and building on one another to deepen students' knowledge and understanding.

TEACHING: Effective teaching requires understanding what students know and need to learn and then challenging and supporting them to learn it well.

LEARNING: By aligning factual knowledge and procedural proficiency with conceptual knowledge, students can become effective learners, reflecting on their thinking and learning from their mistakes.

ASSESSMENT: The tasks teachers select for assessment convey a message to students about what kinds of knowledge and performance are valued. Feedback promotes goal-setting, responsibility, and independence.

TECHNOLOGY: Students can develop a deeper understanding of mathematics with the appropriate use of technology, which can allow them to focus on decision-making, reflection, reasoning, and problem solving.

Our resource correlates to the six Principles and provides teachers with supplementary materials, which can aid them in fulfilling the expectations of each principle. The exercises provided allow for variety and flexibility in teaching and assessment. The topical division of concepts and processes promotes linkage and the building of conceptual knowledge and understanding throughout the student's grade and middle school career. Each of the drill sheet problems help students with their procedural proficiency skills, and offers space for reflection and opportunity for the appropriate use of technology.

Task Sheet 1

1a) The grade 7 class at Whitmore School is planning a **Fair Day – Fun-Raiser** for the last day of school this month. They calculate the cost of supplies for the day will be $250.00. Tickets will be sold at $3.00. Complete the following chart to show how much profit they might make – based on the number of tickets sold. (The profit is based on the number of tickets sold minus the cost of supplies.)

Number of Tickets Sold	Profit
100	
200	
300	
400	
500	

b) Provide the missing labels on the graph, then plot the data from the above chart. (For the **Profit** data, use $200 increments)

Profit ($)

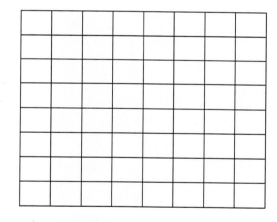

Number of tickets sold

c) Another money-making activity they have planned for the Fair is the **Dunk Tank**. They are hoping to raise at least $200.00 by having the students pay to dunk the vice-principal. If the rental of the tank is $150.00, and they charge $2.00 per participant, how many students will have to participate in order for them to raise $200.00 profit?

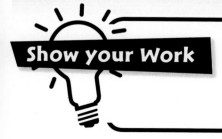

Answer: _____

1 + 2 Task Sheet

Task Sheet 2

2a) Many parts of the world are getting to be quite crowded. Below we have listed ten countries ranked in order of their population (greatest to least). Your task is to match each country with the correct population figure.

China	
United States	
Indonesia	
Mexico	
Vietnam	

Germany	
Egypt	
Iran	
Thailand	
Canada	

82,400,996	234,693,997	85,262,356	33,390,141	80,264,543
65,068,149	1,321,851,888	108,700,891	65,397,521	301,139,947

b) If you add the populations of the nine countries in the above chart that have a smaller population than China, is the combined total greater than China's?

◯ Yes   ◯ No

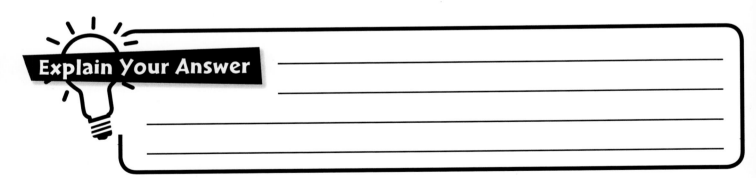

Explain Your Answer

_____

_____

_____

c) The population of the United States is projected to increase by about 1% per year. If that holds true, what would its approximate population be after one year?

i) 346,238,112   ii) 312,367,189   iii) 304,151,346   iv) 301,876,324

Task Sheet 3

3a) Nikki's internet provider charges her a base fee of $26.00 per month for a maximum of 200 online hours. After the 200 hours, she is charged an additional .15¢ per hour. During her first month of usage she was online for a total of 312 hours. What was her bill for the month?

Answer: _____

b) Following this first month, Nikki tried to limit her time on the Internet to reduce her expenses. The following chart illustrates her usage for the next four months:

February	280 hours
March	249 hours
April	415 hours
May	196 hours

What were her total Internet expenses for the months February to May?

i) $155.60   ii) 140.80   iii) 136.60   iv) 184.80

Answer: _____

c) During the first five months that Nikki was with this particular internet provider, what was the average number of hours per month that she was online?

i) 301.4 hours   ii) 256.6 hours   iii) 226.5 hours   iv) 290.4 hours

Use a calculator to complete this chart:

Multiply 4782	
3428	
3107	
234	
9963	

Number and Operations – Task & Drill Sheets CC3312

Task Sheet 4

NAME: _____

4a) Josh got a summer job working at *Pizza Supremo*. The cook's specialty is the macaroni-mushroom pizza, which accounts for 40% of their sales. Their average <u>total</u> daily sales are:

Large	120
Medium	210
Small	315

How many macaroni-mushroom pizzas of each size are sold on the average day?

Macaroni-mushroom Pizza	
Large	
Medium	
Small	

b) A part of their business is also selling pizzas by the slice to walk-in customers. Because their slices are huge, a large pizza is only divided into four slices – however, Josh is not very good at dividing the pizza accurately. Complete the following chart to show how the following pizzas were actually divided (as a decimal of the whole).

Pizza #	Slice 1	Slice 2	Slice 3	Slice 4
1	$^1/_4$	0.23	28%	
2	$^1/_5$	0.30	25%	
3	$^2/_5$	0.15	32%	

c) The making of the famous macaroni-mushroom pizza includes the following ingredients: pizza dough, parmesan cheese, pepperoni, mushrooms, macaroni, tomato sauce, feta cheese, onions and hot peppers. Altogether, the actual cost of ingredients for the pizzas are shown below.

If a large macaroni-mushroom pizza sells for $14.40, a medium for $12.50 and a small $9.50, how much of a profit does *Pizza Supremo* make for each?

Large	$2.10
Medium	$1.80
Small	$1.55

Large	
Medium	
Small	

Task Sheet 5

5a) Grasshoppers have been known to travel great distances in search of food. If a grasshopper hops to a local cornfield 500 yards (457 meters) away at 200 yards (183 meters) per hour, how long will it take him to get to the field and back?

Show your Work

Answer: _____

b) On his way to the cornfield, the grasshopper tumbles into a hole which is 2 yards (1.83 meters) deep! He is able to climb ¼ of a yard (.23 meter) every hour, but then slides back down 1/8 of a yard (.12 meter) because he is so tired. At this rate, how many hours will it take the grasshopper to climb out of the hole?

i) 16 hours   ii) 8 hours   iii) 12 hours   iv) 24 hours

Show your Work

Answer: _____

c) Did you know that there are more than 11,000 species of grasshoppers in the world? This is 4600 more species than the grasshopper's close relative, the katydid. How many species of katydid are there?

_____

d) One type of grasshopper is the lesser migratory grasshopper, which can fly great distances. On a particular trip, one colony flew 128 miles (206 kilometers) to a cornfield near Dubuque. On their return trip they stopped for the summer when they were half way home. What was the total length of their trip?

_____

Task Sheet 6

6a) Janis' dad works at the local hardware store. He asks her to give him a hand this weekend, as they are having a massive sale on all items in the store. Janis' first job is to calculate the sale price on the following items:

i) A baseball mitt. Regular price $45.00. Marked at 20% off.

The sale price = _____

ii) A tricycle. Regular price $30.00. Marked at 30% off.

The sale price = _____

iii) A football. Regular price $36.80. Marked at 25% off.

The sale price = _____

b) The hardware store is having a special sale on golf balls. Janis is asked to paint a big sign which reads, "The more you buy, the more you save." Below the sign is a chart that her dad prepared:

	Cost per ball
Buy 1	$1.25
Buy 2-4	$1.00
Buy 5-9	$0.75
Buy 10-19	$0.50
Buy 20+	

i) If the above rate stays the same, what would the price per ball be for customers purchasing 20 or more? (Complete the chart)

ii) What would the total cost be for a customer buying 15 golf balls?

Answer = _____

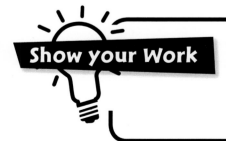

Show your Work

Task Sheet 7

7a) Jordan plays in his town's mixed soccer league. The ratio of boys to girls in the entire league is **21:14**. What percent of the players are girls?

   i) 25%   ii) 50%   iii) 40%   iv) 20%

b) On Jordan's own team, *The Hornets*, the ratio of boys to girls is **4:2**. If there are 15 players on the team, how many are boys?

Answer = _____

c) Jesslyn has quite a sports card collection. When her cousins visited, she gave them ¼ of her collection for 5 valuable rookie cards. Jesslyn now has 65 cards. How many cards did she have before her cousins' visit?

Show your Work

Answer: _____

d) How many phones and planes are needed for the next section of this pattern?

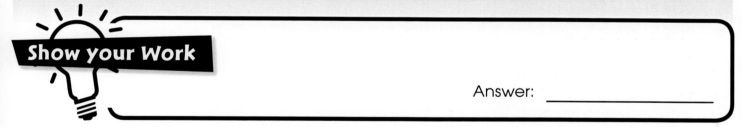

   i)   3 phones, 2 planes   ii)   4 phones, 5 planes

   iii) 2 phones, 3 planes   iv)   3 phones, 4 planes

e) Angie is going to the hardware store to buy some garden tools. While there, she buys a rake for **$12.35**, a shovel for **$16.75**, and a hoe for **$9.89**. How much was her bill?

Answer = _____

Task Sheet 8

8a) Jill recently bought a membership at a local fitness club. During her first week of membership, Jill went to the club every day, spending the following amounts of time (in minutes) there:

- 70, 40, 15, 30, 20, 35, 40

Calculate the mean, the median and the mode.

Show your Work

Mean: _____   Median: _____   Mode: _____

b) Jill found that she enjoyed exercising on the treadmill more than any other piece of equipment. If she spent 40% of her time (in question a) above) on the treadmill, how many minutes did she spend on this piece of equipment?

Answer = _____

c) One of Jill's friends also joined the fitness club. During the same week, she spent a total of 315 minutes at the club. If she missed going on Monday, how many minutes did she average a day, for the remainder of days spent at the fitness club?

Answer = _____

d) The chart on the right shows the fraction of Jill's total time spent on each piece of equipment at the fitness center during her second week. Convert these fractions into percentages.

	Fraction	Percent
Treadmill	$^1/_5$	
Bicycle	$^1/_{10}$	
Stepper	$^1/_4$	
Elliptical	$^3/_{20}$	
HypoCycloidal Trainer	$^3/_{10}$	

Explore With Technology

Outfitting one's own private fitness room can be an expensive project. From a website such as http://www.ebay.com or a catalog, choose four pieces of fitness equipment for your personal gym. Beside each, note the retail price, then total your purchases for the overall cost.

Task Sheet 9

9a) There were 450 people at a sports banquet. Of the guests at the banquet, 1/10 of the people ordered beef, 1/5 ordered shrimp, 2/5 ordered chicken, and the rest ordered the vegetarian meal.

In the table on the right, list the amount of people who ordered the accompanying food.

Beef	
Shrimp	
Chicken	
Vegetarian	

b) Ashley is buying a DVD player with the money she got for her birthday. After doing some comparative shopping, the best deal she could find was one which sold regularly for $66.60, but was on sale for an additional 25% off. What was the total price of the DVD player before taxes?

i) $49.95   ii) $54.35   iii) $47.30   iv) $33.30

c) Brandon and Adam are not only very artistic, but creative as well. They have come up with a fantastic comic book idea which they actually sold to a publisher. The contract they signed for this publishing deal includes a signing bonus plus an amount for every comic book sold. Their potential earnings are illustrated in the chart opposite.

Number of Comics	Earnings ($)
0	2500
2000	2900
4000	3300
6000	3700
8000	4100

How much was their signing bonus and the amount they received per comic book?

Signing Bonus	
Amount per Comic	

d) Madison spent $18.50. She has $32.50 left. How much money did she start with?

Answer = _____

e) Write a story problem for 176 / 12. Solve the problem. What will you do with the remainder?

Task Sheet 10

10a) Amanda's parents have given her the green light for getting a dog for her birthday. They have told her that she has to budget $1000 for the dog and a doghouse. After doing quite a lot of research, she has narrowed her search to three breeds: Bichon Frise, French Bulldog, and an Irish Wolfhound. The following chart breaks down the cost for each dog plus the doghouse.

Dog	Cost of Dog	Cost of Doghouse	Tax (15%)	Total Cost
Bichon Frise	$600	$100		
French Bulldog	$750	$150		
Irish Wolfhound	$800	$175		

Complete the above chart by calculating the tax and totaling the cost for each dog. Which dog(s) come within Amanda's budget?

Show Your Work

b) Before making a final decision, Amanda's dad asks her to also calculate the cost of food for these three breeds. Amanda speaks to the people at the local Kennel Club and is given the following figures for the possible cost of dog food for a month. Calculate the possible cost to Amanda for one year.

Dog	Cost of Dog Food/Month	Cost/Year
Bichon Frise	$20	
French Bulldog	$35	
Irish Wolfhound	$60	

Task Sheet 11

11a) A train ticket costs $65.00 plus 7% state tax. Tamara bought a ticket using one $50 bill and two $10 bills. How much change should Tamara receive?

Show your Work

Answer: _____

b) Mary Jo decided to plant a flower garden this summer. This is what the garden looked like:

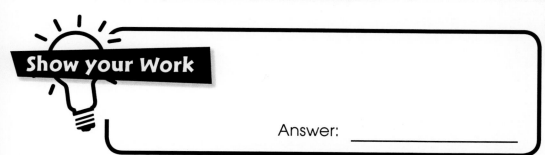

i)   Mary Jo filled 50% of which row?   _____

ii)   Mary Jo filled what % of row B?   _____

iii) How many more percent was row C filled than row A?   _____

Describe how you arrived at your answer for i) above.

_____

_____

c)   If each of the flowers in b) is represented by ⚬ and each dozen flower seeds costs Mary Jo .75¢, how much did she pay for the seeds?

Answer: _____

Task Sheet 12

12a) Caleb and Stephen's results from their last five science tests are shown in the following table:

Caleb	20	21	17	19	21
Stephen	21	21	18	16	18

According to the results presented in this table, calculate the mean scores of both students.

Show your Work

Answer: Caleb: _____   Stephen: _____

b) Using the data presented in the table in 12a), what is the **range** of marks represented by the marks of **both** students?

Range = _____

c) Considering only Caleb's results, what score represents the **mode**?

Mode = _____

d) Considering only Stephen's results, what score represents the **median**?

Median = _____

Explore With Technology   Use a calculator to complete the following:

Multiply 13.705	
24.1	
0.76	
6.02	
99.9	

NAME: _____

Task Sheet 13

13a) List the following rational numbers in order from least to greatest.

0.6   2.7   2 ¹/₂   67%   ³/₄

Show your Work

Answer: _____

b) List the following integers in order from least to greatest.

-4   -12   -26   2   121   -14   17

Answer: _____

c) What number is halfway between ²/₉ and ²/₃?

Show your Work

Answer: _____

d) One number in the following set is not equivalent to the others. Determine which number it is and explain why.

²/₅   40%   ⁸/₂₀   40.0

Show your Work

Answer: _____

Number and Operations – Task & Drill Sheets CC3312

Task Sheet 14

14a) A ball is dropped from a height of **20 feet (6 meters)** above the ground. It bounces to **80%** of its previous height on each bounce. What is the approximate height the ball will bounce on its fourth bounce?

i) 10 feet (3 meters)

ii) 12 feet (3.7 meters)

iii) 8 feet (2.4 meters)

iv) 14 feet (4.3 meters)

b) Jon and several friends buy their lunch at a hot dog stand. A hot dog can be purchased for $2.50 and a soda for .95¢. Jon decides to treat his friends with some birthday money he received from his uncle. If he and his friends bought a total of 5 hot dogs and four colas, how much change would Jon receive from a $20.00 bill?

Show your Work

Answer: _____

c) Do 8^3 and 8×3 mean the same thing?

Explain Your Answer

_____

_____

_____

◯ Yes   ◯ No

d) Courtney earns $12.50 an hour at her summer job. If she works 7.5 hours per day for 5.5 days per week, for 8 weeks, what are her total earnings?

Answer: _____

NAME: _____

Task Sheet 15

15a) The following planets are ranked in order according to approximate diameter from the largest to the smallest. Place the correct diameter beside each planet.

Jupiter	
Saturn	
Uranus	
Neptune	
Earth	
Venus	
Mars	
Mercury	

3 045	88 856	7 519	7 954	4 225	31 752	77 671	30 758	**miles**
4 900	143 000	12 100	12 800	6 800	51 100	125 000	49 500	**kilometers**

b) **What is the difference in kilometers between the largest and smallest planets?**

i) 130 700 (81 213 miles) ii) 138 100 (85 811 miles)

iii) 125 650 (78 075 miles) iv) 14 700 (9 134 miles)

c) **The known moons of the following planets total 164: Saturn, 61; Jupiter 63; Uranus, 27; Neptune __.**

i) How many known moons does Neptune have?

Answer = _____

ii) About what percentage of the total is this?

Answer = _____

Explore With Technology

Use the automatic constant on your calculator to make the calculator count by 5's to 1000. How many seconds does it take your calculator to perform this operation?

Can you calculate how long it would take your calculator to count to one million in this manner?

Drill Sheet 1

1a) **Which of the following fractions is not equivalent to $^{15}/_{45}$?**

    i) $^{10}/_{15}$ ii) $^{1}/_{3}$ iii) $^{4}/_{12}$ iv) $^{30}/_{90}$

b) **The following pattern follows the following rule: double the previous number and add 3.**

    14, 31, 65, 133

    What is the next number in this sequence?

    i) 198   ii) 284   iii) 312   iv) 269   Answer = _____

c) **Compare the following numbers using either > or <.**

    i) 2345 __ 2335   ii) 23.45 __ 23.4   iii) 67234 __ 67234.12   iv) 0.190 __ 0.20

d) **What is the number 10 000 before:**

45 321	
678 424.6	
9 812 345	

e) **Reduce the following to their simplest forms:**

    i) 3/15   ii) 9/27   iii) 2/15   iv) 90/100   v) 75/125

f) **By which number is the pattern decreasing?**

    654 345,   653 345,   652 345,

    i) 100 000   ii) 10 000   iii) 1000   iv) 100   Answer = _____

g) **Which number is closest to 1 000 000**

    i) 978 764   ii) 1 654 231   iii) 1 024 121   iv) 978 745   Answer = _____

NAME: _____

Drill Sheet 2

2a) Which of the following is not a pattern in which a constant is added or subtracted?

    i)   50, 45, 40, 35, 30
    ii)   15, 17, 19, 21, 23
    iii) 6, 10, 14, 18, 22
    iv) 42, 40, 38, 26, 34

b) i) 989 099 + 1 = _____   ii) 23 456 + 100 = _____

iii) 234.3 + 0.01 = _____

c) i) 5^2 = _____   ii) 12^2 = _____   iii) 3^3 = _____   iv) 15^3 = _____   v) 28^3 = _____

d) **Divisor = 7, Quotient = 40, Remainder = 2. What is the dividend?**

i) 282   ii) 287   iii) 285   iv) 28

e) **What answer will have a remainder?**

i) 649 / 8   ii) 490 / 7   iii) 242 / 2   iv) 663 / 3

f) **The population of Mexico is closest to the following number:**

i) 11 000   ii) 11 000 000   iii) 110 000 000   iv) 11 000 000 000

g) **What is the value of this expression -1 + 23/100**

i) – 77/100   ii) – 23/100   iii) - 123/100   iv) - 23/10

h) **What is the missing number in the following pattern below?**

215, 208, 201, ___, 187

Answer = _____

Review A

a) For the following picture, write as many multiplication and division sentences that you can.

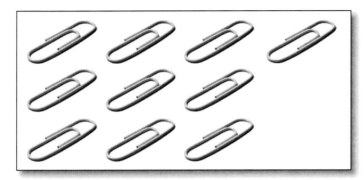 

Answer = _____

b) For each sentence below, write 7 more related sentences (use the same numbers).

i) 4 x 7 = 28   ii) 45 = 9 x 5

Answer i) = _____

Answer ii) = _____

c) There are 15 people in a room. 6 people are wearing socks, 4 people are wearing shoes, and 3 people are wearing both. How many people are in bare feet?

Show your Work

Answer: _____

d) The Revolution Period around the Sun for Earth takes 365 days. If it takes Venus only .62 of this time, approximately how many days is the Revolution Period for the planet Venus?

i) 226 days   ii) 246 days   iii) 198 days   iv) 302 days

NAME: _____

Review B

a) Calculate the mean, mode and median for the following list of numbers.

- 234, 298, 125, 345, 745, 125, 541

Mean	
Mode	
Median	

b) Place a < or > sign between each pair of fractions to indicate which is greater.

i) $^5/_8$ ___ $^7/_8$ ii) $^2/_3$ ___ $^5/_8$ iii) $^1/_3$ ___ $^3/_8$ iv) $^1/_2$ ___ $^5/_8$ v) $^3/_6$ ___ $^3/_7$

c) Replace each blank with the correct digit.

i) 21__ 341 + 8567 = 218908   ii) 23.074 − 12.7__1 = 10.353   iii) 9.2 x 6.__ = 58.88

d) Mrs. Wormstead baked a batch of chocolate chip cookies. Each batch has a total of 15 cookies. Mrs. Wormstead's son, Steadfast, came home and ate 1/3 of this batch. If she then baked three more batches, what is the total number of cookies that Mrs. Wormstead has?

i) 40   ii) 55   iii) 60   iv) 45

e) Meredith finishes a race in 39.761 seconds. Her friend Amanda also ran in the same race. We know the following about Amanda's results:

- The number in the thousandths column is twice that of Meredith's
- The digit in the tens column was six more than Meredith's
- The number in the tenths column was five less than Meredith's

What is Amanda's time?

Answer = _____

f) The following numbers are written in expanded form. Rewrite them in standard form.

i) $4 \times 10^3 + 3 \times 10^2 + 5 \times 10 =$ ii) $7 \times 10^3 + 8 \times 10^2 + 2 \times 10 =$

_____   _____

Review C

a) Your dinner bill at a restaurant comes to **$18.75**. You decide to leave a **15% tip.** What will be your total bill?

Show your Work

Answer: _____

b) Show each of the following fractions as a percent.

i) $4/25$ = ☐   ii) $2/9$ = ☐   iii) $17/19$ = ☐

c) What is the least common multiple (LCM) of the following numbers.

i) 8 and 32 = _____   ii) 15 and 45 = _____

d) $7/9 \times 1/9$ is closest to what integer?

i) 0   ii) 1   iii) 7   iv) 2

e) Samantha works for a moving company. The following table shows her annual salary for the next five years.

Year	Salary
1	28 000
2	30 600
3	33 200
4	35 800
5	38 400

If this continues, what will Samantha's salary be by Year 9?

Answer = _____

NAME: _____

1a) List the following numbers in order from greatest to least. Ex: 1.2, 0.12, 12.1 = 12.1, 1.2, 0.12

i) 2.250, 12.50, 0.225, 225.0 _____

ii) 23 101, 23 011, 32 211, 31 021 _____

b) Write the following numbers in words. Ex: 201 = two hundred one

i) 97 204 = _____

ii) 106 597 = _____

iii) 325 193 = _____

c) Find the value of each percent. Ex: 10% of 60 = 60 x 0.10 = 6

i) 75% of 36   ii) 20% of 85

d) What fractions are shaded? Ex: [▨] = 1 1/2

i)   = _____

ii)   = _____

e) What is the place value of the underlined digit? Ex: 1<u>2</u>3 = tens

i) <u>4</u>567 = _____   ii) 345.7<u>8</u> = _____

Reflection

	Pizza	Drink
Caleb	$3.29	$2.56
Isaac	$4.25	$2.80
Hope	$4.19	$1.99
Ella	$2.79	$1.49

Caleb, Isaac, Hope and Ella each bought a pizza slice and drink. Their choices are shown in the accompanying box. Which person should receive change of <u>about</u> $3.00 from $10.00?

2a) Multiply or divide the following.

i) 7623	ii) 6039	iii) 5199	iv) 8004
× 52	× 75	× 36	× 48

v) 7595 ÷ 49 =   vi) 5775 ÷ 75 =

vii) 4591 × 0.01 =   viii) 2345 × 0.1 =   ix) 7023.3 × 0.001 =

b) Compare the following sets of fractions by writing greater than (>), less than (<) or equal to (=) in the box.   Ex: 2/4 $\boxed{=}$ 1/2

i) 2/3 $\boxed{}$ 1/2   ii) 4/5 $\boxed{}$ 8/10   iii) 2/4 $\boxed{}$ 3/5

c) In a classroom of 36 students, 10 are female. What is the ratio of female to male?
Ex: Ratio of 5 to 9 = 5:9   _____

d) On a hockey team of 18 players, 9 shoot left-handed. What is the ratio of left-handed to right-handed players? _____

e) Solve the following.   Ex: 60 ÷ 5 + 12 x 11 = 12 + 132 = 144

i) 43 + 26 ÷ 2 =   ii) 138 – 12 + (14 + 16 ÷ 4) =

iii) 90 ÷ 10 + 14 x 2 =   iv) 77 ÷ 11 + (13 –7) =

v) (–7) + (–2) =   vi) 14 – (–7) =   vii) 75 + (–50) =

f) Write each number in expanded form.   Ex: 46031 = 40 000 + 6000 + 30 + 1

i) 32 451 = _____

ii) 907 255 = _____

NAME: _____

Minutes

3a) Using the numbers in the centre column below, give numbers that are one thousand more and one hundred less.
Ex: 450 **500** 1550

	100 Less			1000 More
i)		752 609		
ii)		36 268		
iii)		905 992		
iv)		3 168 443		

Least Common Multiple (LCM)

2 and 9
2, 4, 6, 8, 10, 12, 14, 16, 18, 20
9, 18, 27, 36, 45, 54, 63, 72, 81, 90

3 and 7
3, 6, 9, 12, 15, 18, 21, 24, 27, 30
7, 14, 21, 28, 35, 42, 49, 56, 63, 70

b) Calculate the mean, the median and the mode for the following:
Ex: 12, 20, 22, 23, 23   Mean = the average = <u>20</u>   Median = the middle value = <u>22</u>
Mode = the repeated value = 23

i) 62, 88, 44, 71, 62, 68, 81   Mean = _____   Median = _____   Mode = _____

ii) 14, 33, 96, 33, 39, 47, 88   Mean = _____   Median = _____   Mode = _____

c) Solve the following.   Ex: $2^3 = 2 \times 2 \times 2 = 8$

i) $5^2 =$ ii) $7^2 =$ iii) $4^3 =$ iv) $12^3 =$

d) Reduce the following fractions to their simplest forms.
Ex: $4/8 = (4 \div 4) / (8 \div 4) = 1/2$

i) $4/16 =$ ii) $9/27 =$ iii) $3/10 =$ iv) $60/100 =$

e) Compare the following sets of decimals by writing greater than (>), less than (<), or equal to (=) in the box.

i) 6.7 ☐ 6.07   ii) 0.09 ☐ 0.90   iii) 142.010 ☐ 142.01   iv) .051 ☐ .51

f) Find the least common multiple (LCM) of the following numbers.
Ex: 2 and 4 = <u>4</u>   2 = 2, 4, 6, 8, ...   4 = 4, 8, 12, 16, ...

i) 5 and 8 =   ii) 4 and 6 =

g) List the following rational numbers if order from least to greatest.

0.8   3.1   3 ½   90%   7/10   _____

31

4a) **The following chart shows the fraction of Rob's total time spent on each game at a local arcade. Convert these fractions into percentages.**

Ex: 5/10 = 5 ÷ 10 = 0.5 × 100 = 50%

		Fraction	Percent
i)	DrumMania	1/5	
ii)	Time Crisis	3/10	
iii)	The King of Fighters	2/5	
iv)	Galaxian	1/10	

b) **List the following integers in order from least to greatest.**

–6, –13, –26, 9, 131, –1, 26 _____

c) **Which of the following fractions is not equivalent to 7/42?**

i. 1/6   ii. 1/3   iii. 2/12   iv. 21/126

d) **Do 6³ and 6 × 3 mean the same thing?**   YES ☐   NO ☐

e) **What is the number 10 000 before:**

i)	77 561	
ii)	902 518.5	
iii)	10 872 663	

f) **Calculate the following total costs.**

	Bird	Cost of Bird	Cost of Cage	Tax (14%)	Total Cost
Ex:	Peacock	$1900.00	+ $200.00	(x 0.14 =) + $294	= $2,394.00
i)	African Grey Parrot	$1000.00	$120.00		
ii)	Red Macaw	$1200.00	$110.00		

g) **What number comes before 2 000 000?** _____

h) **Replace each blank with the correct digit to make the number sentence correct.**

i) 34 562 + 43 __94 = 77 856   ii) 76 __43 – 45 992 = 30051   iii) 7.__ × 4.6 = 35.42

NAME: _____

5a) Solve the following.

i) 12 + 25 − (18 − 13) × 2 =   ii) 3.4 × 5.6 =   iii) 1230 ÷ 30 =

iv)   4810   v)   7745   vi)   2649   vii)   5012
    × 79   × 80   × 93   × 84

b) Which number is closest to 1 000 000?

i. 987 231   ii. 1 363 497   iii. 1 036 511   iv. 986 999

c) For the following picture, write as many multiplication and division sentences that you can.   Ex: 8 × 4 = 32

Answer: _____

d) Show each of the following fractions as a percent (to the closest whole number).

i) 3/25 =   ii) 17/20 =   iii) 3/5 =   iv) 1/3 =

e) The following numbers are written in expanded form. Rewrite them in standard form.   Ex: $2 \times 10^3 + 5 \times 10^2 + 6 \times 10 + 1 = 2000 + 500 + 60 + 1 = 2561$

i) $7 \times 10^3 + 4 \times 10^2 + 9 \times 10 + 3 =$ ii) $4 \times 10^3 + 1 \times 10^2 + 9 \times 10 + 6 =$

f) Write the following fractions in order from least to greatest.

3/2, 5/4, 6/5 _____

Timed Drill Sheet # 4   NAME: _____

Minutes

6a) **Compare the following numbers using either > or < or =.**

i) 72 341.2 ☐ 72 341.02   ii) 10^3 ☐ 1000

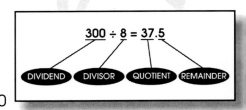

b) **Solve the following.**

i) 162 − 20 × 4 − 3 =   ii) 19 × 6 + 6(12 × 2) =

c) **Which number in the following set is NOT equivalent to the others?**

i. 8.25   ii. 8 1/4   iii. 0.825   iv. 825%

d) **Divisor = 6, Quotient = 52, Remainder = 3. What is the dividend?**

Ex: Divisor = 4, Quotient = 63, Remainder = 2   _____ ÷ 4 = 63.2
63.2 x 4 = 252.8 = Dividend

i. 72   ii. 302   iii. 282   iv. 314

e) **What is the equivalent number to each fraction?**

i) 12/36 = 1/___   ii) 1/4 = ___/64   iii) 9/90 = 18/___   iv) 3/27 = 9/___

f) **Write the place value of the underlined digit.**

i) 450.2̲1 _____   ii) 7̲2 485.44 _____

g) **Write each number in expanded form.**

i) 8136 = _____   ii) 12 697 = _____

h) **What is the least common multiple (LCM) of the following numbers (excluding 1).**

i) 3 and 5 =   ii) 6 and 10 =   iii) 5 and 6 =

Number and Operations – Task & Drill Sheets CC3312

NAME: _____

7a) Solve the following.

   i) (–6) (–4) =   ii) (7) + (–15) =   iii) (–6) (–11) =

b) Calculate the mean, median and mode for the following list of numbers.

149, 296, 461, 345, 149, 333, 108

Mean	
Median	
Mode	

c) What fraction of the creatures below are ants?

 = _____

What is an equivalent fraction of this? _____

d) Multiply the following.

i) 3906
   × 245

ii) 5107
   × 229

iii) 4.68
   × 9.9

iv) 723.8
   × 0.09

e) 8/9 x 5/4 is <u>closest</u> to what integer?   Ex: 3/4 x 7/5 = 21/20 = 1 1/20 = ii. 1

i. 0   ii. 1   iii. 2   iv. 3

Explore With Technology

A very helpful and interesting mathematics website is **Webmath**, found at http://www.webmath.com/

Check out "Math for Everyone." There, you'll find a lot of hands-on practice opportunities like calculating a tip and figuring out a sales price, among others.

8a) Compare the following numbers using either >, or <, or =.

i) 6/7 ☐ 3/4

ii) 7/8 ☐ 2/3

iii) 1/3 ☐ 2/5

iv) 4/3 ☐ 5/4

b) Solve the following.

i) $(44 + 23) - 42 \div 6 =$

ii) $33 + 12 \div 4 + (40 + 15) =$

iii) $(24 \div 8)^2 =$

iv) $4^2 - 12 + (28 - 18)^2 =$

c) Round the following number to the nearest whole number.   Ex: 256.13 = 256

i) 365.12 =

ii) 4199.89 =

iii) 0.513 =

d) Put the following sets of decimals in order from least to greatest.

i) 0.404, 0.66, 1.01, 1.001, 0.110 _____

ii) 5.203, 5.003, 5.030, 3.503 _____

e) Divide the following and round to the nearest hundredth.

i) $567.32 \div 17 =$

ii) $12.672 \div 3.2 =$

iii) $\$652.08 \div 13 =$

iv) $198.80 \div 71 =$

Reflection

You take your two best friends out for lunch. Your treat! The bills come to $14.50, $12.80 and $15.75. If you tip the waitress 15%, what is your total bill (to the closest cent)?

Answer:

9a) Record the following numbers in the accompanying place value charts.

i) 74231.01

Ten Thousands	Thousands	Hundreds	Tens	Ones	Tenths	Hundredths	Thousandths

ii) 60852.09

Ten Thousands	Thousands	Hundreds	Tens	Ones	Tenths	Hundredths	Thousandths

b) Round each number to the nearest 1000.

i) 7652 = _____   ii) 95643 = _____   iii) 816302 = _____

c) Find the value of each percent.

i) 25% of 124 = _____   ii) 90% of 180 = _____   iii) 40% of 126.42 = _____

d) Multiply the following.

i) $75.45
   × 35

ii) 653.89
   × 5.4

iii) $231.75
   × 105

iv) 22.7
   × 0.06

e) Divide the following.

i) 0.002 ÷ 100 = _____   ii) 7.89 ÷ 1000 = _____   iii) 32.678 ÷ 100 =

f) Write the next numbers in the following patterns.

i) 716, 666, 616, ____, ____   ii) 11, ____, 33, ____, 55   iii) 90.3, 89.9, 89.5, ____, ____

g) Reduce the following fractions to their lowest terms.

i) 12/60 = ____   ii) 85/130 = ____   iii) 80/88 = ____

h) What percentage of the vegetables below are corn? _____

10a) Solve the following.   Ex: 2 x 1/4 x 2/8 = 2/4 x 2/8 = 4/32 or 1/8

i) 3 × 1/3 × 2/5 =

ii) 5 × 1/3 × 3/12 =

iii) (16.2 + 0.8) × 2 =

iv) 18 ÷ 2.4 =

v) 23.23 + 171.34 + 2.9 + 0.002 =

vi) (–12) (–8) + (–6) =

b) Write the place value of the underlined digit.

i) 2781.02<u>1</u> _____

ii) <u>9</u>9 724.281 _____

c) Show each of the following fractions as a percent.

i) 9/45 =

ii) 20/200 =

iii) 8/25 =

iv) 16/400 =

d) Divisor = 9, Dividend = 842, Remainder = 5. What is the quotient? _____

e) Divisor = 8, Dividend = 1251, Remainder = 3. What is the quotient? _____

Reflection

Paul was hired by the local golf course to retrieve balls in the evening from a few spots on the course. It is agreed that Paul will receive 0.25¢ per ball. During his first week, Paul earned $180.00. Calculate the number of golf balls retrieved for each day in the chart below.

	Mon.	Tues.	Wed.	Thurs.	Fri.	TOTAL
Amt Earned	$32.00	$20.50	$60.75	$55.25	$11.50	$180.00
Balls Retrieved						

11a) Solve the following.

Ex: $1/2 \div 1/5 = 1/2 \times 5/1 = 5/2$ or $2\ 1/2$

i) $232 \times 10^2 =$

ii) $76.29 \times 10^1 =$

iii) $(12 + 9)^2 - (8 \times 3) =$

iv) $(3.2 + 6.43) - (12 - 8) =$

v) $4/5 \div 3/8 =$

vi) $9/10 \div 7/8 =$

b) Put the following sets of numbers in order from greatest to least.

i) 17.001, 1.701, 17.01, 71.010 _____

ii) 0.023, 0.230, 0.0023, 0.1023 _____

c) Jasmine works at a local restaurant as a waitress. As she improves her waitressing skills the tips she receives from customers have increased accordingly. Her tips for the last three days are shown in the chart below. If her tips increase at this rate, what will she probably receive in tips on Day 4?

Day	Tips
1	$16.00
2	$22.00
3	$28.00
4	

d) Write the improper fraction equivalent for each mixed number.

Ex: $4\ 3/5 = ((5 \times 4) + 3)/5 = 23/5$

i) $3\ 1/2 =$

ii) $7\ 7/8 =$

iii) $2\ 9/10 =$

iv) $17\ 2/3 =$

v) $6\ 3/4 =$

vi) $12\ 2/5 =$

e) Find the value of each percent.

i) 18% of 3200

ii) 44% of 9300

12a) Solve the following.

i) $43.65
    ×   98

ii) 2.891
     × 0.2

iii) $336.78
      ×   369

iv) (3.8 + 5.8) ÷ (6.8 – 3.8) =   v) (7.5 – 0.25) × (6.22 + 4.01) =

b) Write a fraction for each decimal.

Ex: 0.450 = 450/1000 = 9/20
Ex: 1.222 = 1 2/9

i) 0.125 =   ii) 0.250 =   iii) 1.333 =

iv) 0.90 =   v) 3.8 =   vi) 75.75 =

c) Round the following number to the nearest 1000.

i) 77 643.2 =   ii) 1 256 380 =   iii) 555 =

d) Write the number 90 090 in words. _____

e) In the chart below, five math scores (out of 25) are listed for Eric and Maggie. For each student, calculate the mean, median and mode.

	Test 1	Test 2	Test 3	Test 4	Test 5	Mean	Median	Mode
Eric	22	19	25	22	17			
Maggie	21	23	17	22	17			

Explore With Technology

Use a calculator to complete the following. Keep in mind the proper <u>order of operations</u>!

17 234 + 234.1 – (32 – 20)² × 7

NAME: _____

13a) Samantha planted **6 cedars** and **9 birch trees** in her backyard. What is the ratio of cedars to birch trees?

Ex: Ratio of 5 to 9 = 5 : 9

b) Find the prime factors of the following numbers. Ex: $12 = 2 \times 2 \times 3$

i) 18 =   ii) 30 =

iii) 36 =   iv) 72 =

c) What is the greatest common factor of the following pairs of numbers?

Ex: 12 and 16 = 4   (12 ÷ 4 = 3; 16 ÷ 4 = 4)

i) 12 and 18   ii) 15 and 36

d) If the sales tax is **7%**, what is the <u>total</u> cost of items priced as follows (to the nearest cent)?

i) $24.00   ii) $52.60

e) Solve the following.

i) 2/3 x 4/5 =   ii) 7/8 ÷ 3/10 =

iii) 3/4 + 7/8 =   iv) 6/7 – 2/3 =

v) (–3) + (4)(–2) =   vi) (–2) (–18) – 6^2 =

vii) 75 – (–3)(–6) =   viii) $9^2 + 3^3$ =

ix) $175.50
       ×   38
    [   ]

x)   90.091
      × 0.2
    [   ]

xi) $3456.04
      ×   216
    [   ]

xii)   0.9002
       × 0.77
    [   ]

14a) Write the place value of the underlined digit.

i) 341893.23<u>4</u> = _____   ii) <u>6</u>39 745.116 = _____

b) Use >, <, or = to compare the pairs of numbers below.

i) 7762.661 ☐ 7762.0661   ii) 996.080 ☐ 996.08

c) Solve the following.

i) 567.341 x 100 =   ii) 43 x 10³ =

iii) 0.00023 x 0.001 =   iv) 10² x 10¹ =

v) 144 ÷ 12 =   vi) 72 ÷ 8 =

vii) 99 ÷ 11 =   viii) 12 x 11 =

d) Write the following numbers using words.   Ex: 32.6 = <u>thirty two decimal six</u>

i) 325.23 = _____

ii) 277 359 = _____

e) Write the <u>expanded form</u> for each of the following numbers.   Ex: 10.12 = <u>10 + 0.1 + 0.02</u>

i) 67 892 = _____   ii) 78 401.96 = _____

f) For the following picture, write as many multiplication and division sentences that you can.

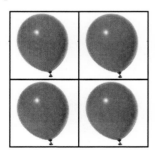
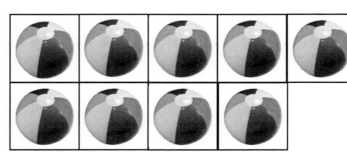

_____

_____

_____

_____

_____

g) Find the value of each percent:

i) 60% of 90   ii) 32% of 200

15a) Record the following numbers in the accompanying place value charts.

i) 56.024	Ten Thousands	Thousands	Hundreds	Tens	Ones	Tenths	Hundredths	Thousandths

ii) 90023.846	Ten Thousands	Thousands	Hundreds	Tens	Ones	Tenths	Hundredths	Thousandths

b) What fractions are shaded?

i) ▭▭▭ ▭▭▭ ▭▭▭ ▭▢▢ = _____

ii) ▭▭▭▭ ▭▭▭▭ ▭▭▭▭ ▭▭▭▢ = _____

c) Solve the following.

i) $701 \times 10^3 =$ ii) $0.034 \times 10^1 =$ iii) $12.2 \times 0.001 =$

iv) $8(0.03 \times 1.2) - (6 \times 0.02) =$ v) $(0.04 \times 3.4) + (17 \times 0.02) =$

vi) $2/3 \div 7/9 =$ vii) $5/3 \div 9/11 =$

d) Josh has played baseball for the past four summers. His home run totals for these four years were; 12, 17, 23 and 19. What is the mean number of home runs (to the nearest whole number)? _____

e) Four hundred students attend General Brock Public School. Twenty percent had perfect attendance. How many students had perfect attendance? _____

f) Write the mixed number for each of the following.   Ex: 10/3 = 3 1/3

i) $13/6 =$ ii) $19/2 =$ iii) $43/12 =$

Timed Drill Sheet # 10   NAME: _____

16a) What is the <u>first step</u> in the order of operations for the following?   Ex: $3^2 + 2 - 1 = \underline{3^2}$

i) $12 + 14 \div 2 - 7 \times 8$ _____

ii) $16 + 14 - 3(2 \times 6) \div 4$ _____

b) If the weather report says that there is a **60%** chance of rain, what fraction represents this amount ?   _____

c) Write the improper fraction equivalent for each mixed number.

i) $7\ 1/3 =$ ii) $12\ 3/4 =$ iii) $1\ 6/7 =$

d) Write greater than (>), less than (<), or equal to (=) in the box.

i) 7041.22 ☐ 7041.220 ii) 23501.0023 ☐ 23051.0032

e) Solve the following.

i) $2/3 \div 3/4 =$ ii) $0.42 \times 0.78 =$

iii) $0.032 \times 10^3 =$ iv) $5/6 \times 8/10 =$

v) $0.9832 \div 0.05 =$ vi) $3/4 \div 1/2 =$

vii) $12\ (2 + 12) - 10^2 =$ viii) $12 + 10 - 5 \times 3 + (6 \times 13) =$

ix) $(2 + 12 \div 4)^2 =$ x) $1/8 \times 1/2 \times 2/3 =$

f) For each pair of numbers below, <u>circle</u> the one that is **LARGER**.

i) 100 or 10^3 ii) $2/3$ or 0.87 iii) 60% or $4/5$

NAME: _____

17a) Calculate the mean, the median and the mode for the following.

i) 24, 18, 36, 40, 24, 16, 31

ii) 50, 42, 66, 44, 66, 80, 58

> 21, 23, 23, 24, 26, 27, 29, 30, 31
>
> Mean = **26**
>
> Median = **26**
>
> Mode = **23**

b) Solve the following:

i) $7^2 + 3^2 =$　　ii) $9^2 =$　　iii) $5^3 =$　　iv) $8^3 =$

v) $334.7 \times 0.01 =$　　vi) $38912.1 \times 0.1 =$　　vii) $36112 \times 10^2 =$

c) Reduce the following to their simplest forms:

i) $7/49 =$　　ii) $9/81 =$　　iii) $6/120 =$　　iv) $4/100 =$

d) Write each number in expanded form.

i) 237 650 = _____

ii) 2 387 659 = _____

e) Place the correct number in each of the boxes in the following questions to make this number sentence correct.

i) $143 - \boxed{} = 67$　　ii) $9 \times \boxed{} = 72$　　iii) $212 + \boxed{} = 511$

f) Write the next two numbers in the following patterns.

i) 144, 132, 120, _____, _____　　ii) 14, 28, 42, _____, _____

Number and Operations – Task & Drill Sheets CC3312

Review A

a) List the following numbers in order from greatest to least:

17.34, 21.009, 1.734, 2.1009, 0.1734 _____

b) Write the following number in words.

86 356 _____

c) Determine:

i) 40% of 24 _____

ii) 25% of 120 _____

d) Write the place value of the underlined digit.

i) 5902.5 = _____   ii) 2548.23 = _____

e) Write the following number in expanded form.

134 691 = _____

f) Multiply the following.

i) 3518	ii) 804.3	iii) $32.78	iv) 5397
× 78	× 34	× 51	× 0.02

g) In Rene's swim team, 12 of the 19 members are girls. What is the ratio of girls to boys on her swim team? _____

h) Find the missing number in the fraction equivalents.

i) 4/5 = ___/25   ii) 1/2 = ___/24   iii) 12/48 = 1/___

NAME: _____

Review B

a) What is the number 10 000 before the following:

i)	80 252	
ii)	952 873.6	

b) Multiply the following.

i) 5902	ii) $53.90	iii) 765.1	iv) 56.01
× 245	× 376	× 23.5	× 3.7

c) Calculate the mean, median and mode for the following list of numbers.

390, 440, 280, 782, 440, 336, 146

Mean	
Median	
Mode	

d) Record the following number in the accompanying place value chart.   29 064.013

Ten Thousands	Thousands	Hundreds	Tens	Ones	Tenths	Hundredths	Thousandths

e) Solve the following.

i) $1/3 \times 4/5 =$

ii) $7/8 \div 1/4 =$

iii) $7 \times 1/5 \times 2/7 =$

iv) $2/3 \div 1/8 \times 1/2 =$

v) $6.2 \times 10^2 =$

vi) $0.002 \times 10^3 =$

NAME: _____

Review C

a) Write 3 453 629 in words.

_____

b) Reduce the following to their simplest forms.

i) 5/25 _____   ii) 7/42 _____   iii) 21/63 _____   iv) 12/60 _____

c) Solve the follwing.

i) $6^2 + 9^2 =$ ii) $12^2 =$ iii) $7^3 =$ iv) $8^2 + 50 =$

v) 772.91 x 0.01 =   vi) $0.8643 \times 10^2 =$

vii) $10 (15 \div 5)^2 =$ viii) $112 - 60 - (16 \div 4 + 8) + 7 =$

ix) $(7 + 12) (8 \times 12) =$ x) $1/6 \times 5/6 =$

xi) $3/4 \div 7/9 =$ xii) $3 1/2 \times 6/11 =$

d) Find the value of each percent.

i) 40% of 160 =   ii) 120% of 50 =

e) Write the improper fraction equivalent for each mixed number.

i) 9   1/2 =   ii) 10   2/3 =   iii) 7   7/8 =

7.

a) iii) 40%

b) 10

c) 80

d) iv) 3 phones, 4 planes

e) $38.99

(15)

6.

a)
i) $36
ii) $21
iii) $27.60

b) i) .25¢
ii) 15 x .50¢ = $7.50

(14)

4.

a)
Large – 48;
Medium – 84;
Small – 126

b)
1 - .24
2 - .25
3 - .13

c)
Large - $12.30
Medium - $10.70
Small - $7.95

(12)

5.

a) 5 hours

b) 16 hours -
he only progresses
1/8 yd/hr.
(.12 meters/hr)

c) 6400

d)
128 + 64=192 miles
(206 + 103 = 309
kilometers)

(13)

3.

a) 112 x .15¢ =
$16.80 + $26.00 =
$42.80

b) i) 155.60
February 280 hours
$12.00
March 249 hours
$7.35
April 415 hours
$32.25
May 196 hours 0
Monthly fee x 4
$104.00
TOTAL i) $155.60

c) iv) 280 + 249 +
415 + 196 + 312 =
1452 / 5 = 290.4
hours

3428 - 16392696
3107 - 14857674
234 - 1118988
9963 - 47643066

(11)

2.

a)
China 1,321,851,888
United States 301,139,947
Indonesia 234,693,997
Mexico 108,700,891
Vietnam 85,262,356

Germany 82,400,996
Egypt 80,264,543
Iran 65,397,521
Thailand 65,068,149
Canada 33,390,141

b) NO - The total
of the other 9
countries is 1 056
318 541 – smaller
than China's
population.

c) iii) 304,151,346

(10)

1.

a)
100 - $50
200 - $350
300 - $650
400 - $950
500 - $1250

b)

c)
175 (Various ways of
arriving at this answer
i.e. 2x – 150 = 200
2x = 200 + 150
x = 175

(9)

14.

a) iii) 8 feet (2.4 meters) Reduce by 20% with each bounce. 20 – 16 – 12.8 – 10.24 – 8.192

b) $20.00 – ($2.50 x 5 = $12.50)-(.95¢ x 4 = $3.80) = $3.70

c) No.
8^3 = 8 x 8 x 8 = 512 while 8 x 3 = 24

d) $12.50 x 7.5 x 5.5 x 8 = $4125.00

⋯22⋯

13.

a) 0.6, 67%. ¾, 2 ½, 2.7 – convert to decimals ~ .6, .67, .75, 2.5, 2.7

b) -26, -14, -12, -4, 2, 17, 121

c) 4/9 ~ halfway between 2/9 and 6/9

d) 40.0 is not equivalent -
2/5 = .40
40% = .40
8/20 = .40
40.0 = 40.00

⋯21⋯

11.

a) $65 x 1.07 = $69.55
$70.00 - $69.55 = .45¢

b) i) E
ii) 10%
iii) 40%

c) There are 36 flowers (3 dozen) - .75¢ x 3 = $2.25

⋯19⋯

10.

a) $105 $805
$135 $1035
$146.25 $1121.25

• The Bichon Frise came within her $1000 budget

b) Bichon Frise - $240.00
French Bulldog - $420.00
Irish Wolfhound - $720.00

⋯18⋯

12.

a) Caleb – 19.6
Stephen – 18.8

b) 5

c) 21

d) 18

⋯20⋯

9.

a) Beef 45; Shrimp 90; Chicken 180; Vegetarian 135.

b) i) $49.95

c) Signing bonus is $2500. Amount per comic = $400 / 2000 = .20¢

8.

a) Mean = 35.71
Median = 35
Mode = 40

b) 100 min.

c) 315 / 6 = 52.5 min.

d) Treadmill – 20%; Bicycle – 10%; Stepper – 25%; Elliptical – 15%; HypoCycloidal – 30%

d) $18.50 + 32.50 = $51.00

e) Answers will vary.

⋯17⋯

⋯16⋯

Drill Sheet 1

a) i) 10/15

b) iv) 269

c) i) >
ii) >
iii) <
iv) <

d) 35321
668424.6
9802345

e) i) 1/5
ii) 1/3
iii) 2/15
iv) 9/10
v) 3/5

f) iii) 1000

g) i) 978 764

(24)

Drill Sheet 2

a)
iv) 42, 40, 38, 26, 34

b) i) 989 100
ii) 23 556
iii) 234.31

c) i) 25
ii) 144
iii) 27
iv) 3375
v) 784

d) i) 282

e) i) 649 / 8 = 81 r1
ii) 490 / 7 = 70
iii) 242 / 2 = 121
iv) 663 / 3 = 221

f) iii) 110 000 000

g) i) – 77/100

h) 194

(25)

Review A

a) Answers may vary.

b) Answers may vary.

c) 2

d) i) 226 days

(26)

Review B

a) mean = 344.71;
mode = 125;
median = 298

b) i) < ii) > iii) <
iv) < v) >

c) i) 0 ii) 2 iii) 4

d) ii) 55

e) 45.262

f) i) 4,350 ii) 7,820

(27)

Review C

a) $21.56

b) i) 16%
ii) 22%
iii) 89%

c) i) 32 ii) 45

a) i) 0

e) $48 800

EZ✔

(28)

a) Jupiter
88 856 (143 000km)
Saturn
77 671 (125 000km)
Uranus
31 752 (51 100km)
Neptune
30 758 (49 500km)
Earth
7 954 (12 800km)
Venus
7 519 (12 100km)
Mars
4 225 (6 800km)
Mercury
3 045 (4 900km)

b) ii) 138 100
kilometers
(85 811 miles)

c) i) 13
ii) 7.9%

(23)

6.

a) B=15
b) C=25
c) B=44
d) C=48
e) i) 5/3
 ii) 10/9
 iii) 2/1
 iv) 3/5
f) i) 3 8/9
 ii) 11 9/16
g) 540

6A

5.

a) i) 7
 ii) 3
 iii) 11
b) 8
c) i) 64 000
 ii) 4 000
 iii) 1000
d) i) 1
 ii) 1 1/8
 iii) 1 2/3
e) 17
f) Mean = 17.6
 Mode = 12
 Median = 14

5A

4.

a) $75 × 1.1 = $82.50
 × .80 = $66.00 × 1.3 = $85.80
b) 3 and 5
c) i) >
 ii) <
 iii) <
 iv) >
d) i) 12/21
 ii) 6/30
 iii) 3/5
 iv) 49/56
e) Charles -
 Charles ~ 32/40
 Barbara ~ 30/40

4A

3.

a) 75% 3/4
 0.30 3/10
 0.40 40%
 85% 85/100 or 17/20
 0.15 15/100 or 3/20
 125% 1 1/4
b) i) 25%
 ii) 40%
c) $20.00 – 16.41 = $3.59

3A

2.

a) Between noon and 1:00 p.m. (Then he travels only 33 miles (53 km), compared to 50+ miles (80 km.) at all other times.)
b) 9+8+7+65+4+3+2+1 = 99
c) $678 - $240.00 = $438 / $36.50 = 12 hours.
d) $212.50 × 6 = $1275 + $375 + $408.25 = $2058.25

2A

1.

a) Convert to decimals. Jenna has .40 left, Charmaine .30 left, Rhonda .28 left and Aubrey .35 left. Therefore Jenna has the most left.
b) Laurie – Bert – Ken – Shawn
c) Answers will vary (i.e. 400 – 24 = 376)
d) 310 m/hr (499 km/hr)

1A

1.

a)
i) 225.0, 12.50, 2.250, 0.225
ii) 32 211, 31 021, 23 101, 23 011

b)
i) ninety-seven thousand two hundred four
ii) one hundred six thousand five hundred ninety-seven
iii) three hundred twenty-five thousand one hundred ninety-three

c)
i) 27   ii) 17

d)
i) 2 1/4
ii) 3 2/3

e)
i) thousands
ii) hundredths

29

2.

a)
i) 396 396
ii) 452 925
iii) 187 164
iv) 384 192
v) 155   vi) 77
vii) 45.91
viii) 234.5
ix) 7.0233

b)
i) >   ii) =   iii) <

c)
10:26

d)
9:9

e)
i) 56   ii) 144
iii) 37   iv) 13
v) –9   vi) 21   vii) 25

f)
i) 30 000 + 2000 + 400 + 50 + 1
ii) 900 000 + 7000 + 200 + 50 + 5

30

3.

a)
i) 752 509, 753 609
ii) 36 168, 37 268
iii) 905 892, 906 992
iv) 3 168 343, 3 169 443

b)
i) Mean = 68
Median = 68
Mode = 62
ii) Mean = 50
Median = 39
Mode = 33

c)
i) 25   ii) 49
iii) 64   iv) 1728

d)
i) 1/4   ii) 1/3
iii) 3/10   iv) 3/5

e)
i) >   ii) <
iii) =   iv) <

f)
i) 40   ii) 12

g)
7/10, 0.8, 90%,
3.1, 3 1/2

31

4.

a)
i) 20%
ii) 30%
iii) 40%
iv) 10%

b)
–26, –13, –6, –1, 9, 26, 131

c)
ii. 1/3

d) NO

e)
i) 67 561
ii) 892 518.5
iii) 10 862 663

f)
i) $1276.80
ii) $1493.40

g)
1 999 999

h)
i) 43 294
ii) 76 043
iii) 7.7

32

5.

a)
i) 27
ii) 19.04
iii) 41
iv) 379 990
v) 619 600
vi) 246 357
vii) 421 008

b) i.

c)
8 × 4 = 32, 4 × 8 = 32,
32 ÷ 8 = 4, 32 ÷ 4 = 8

d)
i) 12%   ii) 85%
iii) 60%   iv) 33%

e)
i) 7493   ii) 4196

f)
6/5, 5/4, 3/2

33

6.

a)
i) >   ii) =

b)
i) 79   ii) 258

c) iii.

d) iv.

e)
i) 3   ii) 16
iii) 180   iv) 81

f)
i) tenths
ii) ten thousands

g)
i) 8000 + 100 + 30 + 6
ii) 10 000 + 2000 + 600 + 90 + 7

h)
i) 15   ii) 30   iii) 30

34

14.

a) i) thousandths
ii) hundred thousands

b) i) > ii) =

c) i) 56734.1 ii) 43 000
iii) 0.0000023 iv) 1000
v) 12 vi) 9
vii) 9 viii) 132

d) i) three hundred twenty-five decimal twenty-three
ii) two hundred seventy-seven thousand three hundred fifty-nine

e) i) 60 000 + 7000 + 800 + 90 + 2
ii) 70 000 + 8000 + 400 + 1 + 0.9 + 0.06

f) 4 x 9 = 36, 9 x 4 = 36, 36 ÷ 9 = 4, 36 ÷ 4 = 9

g) i) 54 ii) 64

(42)

13.

a) 6:9

b) i) 2 x 3 x 3
ii) 3 x 2 x 5
iii) 3 x 3 x 2 x 2
iv) 2 x 2 x 2 x 3 x 3

c) i) 6 ii) 3

d) i) $25.68 ii) $56.28

e) i) 8/15
ii) 70/24 or 2 11/12
iii) 13/8 or 1 5/8
iv) 4/21 v) –11
vi) 0 vii) 57
viii) 108
ix) $6669.00
x) 18.0182
xi) $746 504.64
xii) 0.693154

(41)

12.

a) i) $4277.70
ii) 0.5782
iii) $124 271.82
iv) 3.2
v) 74.1675

b) i) 1/8 ii) 1/4
iii) 1 1/3 iv) 9/10
v) 3 4/5 vi) 75 3/4

c) i) 78 000
ii) 1 256 000
iii) 1000

d) ninety thousand ninety

e)

	Mean	Median	Mode
Eric	21	22	22
Maggie	20	21	17

(40)

10.

a) i) 6/15 or 2/5
ii) 15/36 or 5/12
iii) 34 iv) 7.5
v) 197.472 vi) 90

b) i) thousandths
ii) ten thousands

c) i) 20% ii) 10%
iii) 32% iv) 4%

d) 93

e) 156

(38)

11.

a) i) 23200 ii) 762.9
iii) 417 iv) 5.63
v) 32/15 or 2 2/15
vi) 72/70 or 1 1/35

b) i) 71.010, 17.01,
17.001, 1.701
ii) 0.230, 0.1023,
0.023, 0.0023

c) $34.00

d) i) 7/2 ii) 63/8
iii) 29/10 iv) 53/3
v) 27/4 vi) 62/5

e) i) 576 ii) 4092

(39)

9.

a) i)

Ten Thousands	Thousands	Hundreds	Tens	Ones	Tenths	Hundredths	Thousandths
7	4	2	3	1	0	1	0

i)

Ten Thousands	Thousands	Hundreds	Tens	Ones	Tenths	Hundredths	Thousandths
6	0	8	5	2	0	9	0

b) i) 8000 ii) 96 000
iii) 816 000

c) i) 31 ii) 162 iii) 50.568

d) i) $2640.75
ii) 3531.006
iii) $24333.75
iv) 1.362

e) i) 0.00002
ii) 0.00789
iii) 0.32678

f) i) 566, 516
ii) 22, 44
iii) 89.1, 88, 7

g) i) 1/5 ii) 17/26
iii) 10/11

h) 40%

(37)

7.

a) i) 24 ii) –8 iii) 66

b) Mean - 263
Median - 296
Mode - 149

c) 4/10, 2/5

d) i) 956 970
ii) 1 169 503
iii) 46.332
iv) 65.142

e) ii.

(35)

8.

a) i) > ii) >
iii) < iv) >

b) i) 60 ii) 91
iii) 9 iv) 104

c) i) 365 ii) 4200 iii) 1

d) i) 0.110, 0.404, 0.66,
1.001, 1.01
ii) 3.503, 5.003,
5. 030, 5.203

e) i) 33.37 ii) 3.96
iii) $50.16 iv) 2.80

(36)

Review C

a) three million four hundred fifty-three thousand six hundred twenty-nine

b)
i) 1/5   ii) 1/6
iii) 1/3   iv) 1/5

c)
i) 117   ii) 144
iii) 343   iv) 114
v) 7.7291   vi) 86.43
vii) 90   viii) 47
ix) 1824   x) 5/36
xi) 27/28
xii) 42/22 or 1 10/11

d)
i) 64   ii) 60

e)
i) 19/2
ii) 32/3
iii) 63/8

Review B

a)
i) 70 252   ii) 942 873.6

b)
i) 1 445 990
ii) $20 266.40
iii) 17 979.85
iv) 207.237

c)
Mean - 402,
Median - 390,
Mode - 440

d)
i)

Ten Thousands	Thousands	Hundreds	Tens	Ones	Tenths	Hundredths	Thousandths
2	9	0	6	4	0	1	3

e)
i) 4/15
ii) 28/8 or 3 1/2
iii) 2/5
iv) 16/6 or 2 2/3
v) 620
vi) 2

Review A

a)
21.009, 17.34, 2.1009,
1.734, 0.1734

b)
eighty-six thousand
three hundred fifty-six

c)
i) 9.6
ii) 30

d)
i) tenths
ii) hundreds

e)
100 000 + 30 000 +
4000 + 600 + 90 + 1

f)
i) 274 404
ii) 27 346.2
iii) $ 1671.78
iv) 107.94

g)
12:7

h)
i) 20   ii) 12   iii) 4

17.

a)
i) Mean - 27;
Median - 24;
Mode - 24
ii) Mean - 58;
Median - 58;
Mode - 66

b)
i) 58
ii) 81
iii) 125
iv) 512
v) 3.347
vi) 3891.21
vii) 3611200

c)
i) 1/7   ii) 1/9
iii) 1/20   iv) 1/25

d)
i) 200 000 + 30 000 +
7000 + 600 + 50
ii) 2 000 000 +
300 000 + 80 000 +
7000 + 600 + 50 + 9

e)
i) 76   ii) 8
iii) 299

f)
i) 108, 96   ii) 56, 70

16.

a)
i) 14 ÷ 2 or 7 × 8
ii) (2 × 6)

b)
60/100 = 3/5

c)
i) 22/3
ii) 51/4
iii) 13/7

d)
i) =   ii) >

e)
i) 8/9   ii) 0.3276
iii) 32   iv) 2/3
v) 19.664   vi) 1 1/2
vii) 68   viii) 85
ix) 25   x) 1/24

f)
i) 10³   ii) 0.87   iii) 4/5

15.

a)
i)

Ten Thousands	Thousands	Hundreds	Tens	Ones	Tenths	Hundredths	Thousandths
0	0	0	5	6	0	2	4

i)

Ten Thousands	Thousands	Hundreds	Tens	Ones	Tenths	Hundredths	Thousandths
9	0	0	2	3	8	4	6

b)
i) 3 1/3   ii) 3 3/4

c)
i) 701 000
ii) 0.34
iii) 0.0122
iv) 0.168
v) 0.476
vi) 18/21 or 6/7
vii) 55/27 or 2 1/27

d) 18
e) 80
f)
i) 2 1/6
ii) 9 1/2
iii) 3 7/12

EZ✔

1.

a) i) 17.021, 17.012, 1.7021, 1.7012
ii) 0.1053, 0.0353, 0.0053, 0.0035

b) i) two hundred thirty-four thousand eight hundred twelve
ii) one million three hundred forty-nine thousand twenty-five

c) 8:16

d) i) 30 ii) 86
iii) 154 iv) 47

e) 50%

f) i) = ii) < iii) >

g) i) Mean = 50,
Median = 55,
Mode = 43
ii) Mean = 107,
Median = 107,
Mode = 118

1A

2.

a) i) 11 000 ii) 1000
iii) 173 000

b) i) 10 000 + 5000 + 600 + 3
ii) 200 000 + 60 000 + 3000 + 400 + 90 + 9

c) 9 × 5 = 45, 5 × 9 = 45,
45 ÷ 9 = 5, 45 ÷ 5 = 9

d) i) 264 883 ii) $1658.25
iii) 349.32 iv) $18 523.80

e) i) 21 ii) 10 iii) 30

f) i) 64 ii) 148
iii) 64 iv) 222

2A

3.

a) i) 30% ii) 10%
iii) 20% iv) 40%

b)

i)

Ten Thousands	Thousands	Hundreds	Tens	Ones	Tenths	Hundredths	Thousandths
4	5	6	9	1	0	0	3

iii)

Ten Thousands	Thousands	Hundreds	Tens	Ones	Tenths	Hundredths	Thousandths
7	0	8	3	4	3	2	1

c) i) 9/2 ii) 25/3
iii) 27/5 iv) 75/8
v) 51/7 vi) 95/9

d) i) 375 ii) 108

e) i) 2/5 ii) 2/5 iii) 3/5

f) i) 6.2 ii) 2370 iii) 4500

3A

4.

a) i) 1/5 ii) 1/9 iv) 1/9
iii) 1/12

b) i) $15 927.12
ii) 54.5314
iii) $916555.50
iv) 0.677124

c) i) 154, 165 ii) 69, 45

d) i) 864 ii) 6
iii) 25 iv) 768
v) 1/6 vi) 15/32
vii) 0.539 viii) 2340
ix) 98000 x) $5.00
xi) 6/40 or 3/20
xii) 9/14

4A

5.

a) i) 18 ii) 32
iii) 24 iv) 45

b) i) = ii) > iii) >

c) i) hundredths
ii) hundred thousands

d) 900 000 + 80 000 +
2000 + 700 + 50 + 4

e) i) 5 ii) 8

f) i) 25% ii) 5%
iii) 28% iv) 38%

g) 133

h) 50

5A

6.

a) i) 34.67
ii) 2.90
iii) 18.11

b) i) $1103.54
ii) 2254
iii) $22415.25
iv) 0.142686
v) 10/6 or 1 2/3 vi) 10.8
vii) 18/56 or 9/28
viii) 18/30 or 3/5

c) i) sixty-five thousand
two hundred thirty-four
ii) one hundred
seventy-eight
thousand nine
hundred thirty-five

d) 3 2/3

e) i) 2 × 2 × 2 × 3
ii) 2 × 2 × 3 × 5
iii) 2 × 2 × 7

6A

a) Determine the following mixed fraction.

b) Round each of the following numbers to the nearest thousand.

i)   ii)   iii)

c) Place either > or < between the following pairs of fractions or decimals to indicate which is greater.

i) ___ □ ___   ii) ___ □ ___   iii) ___ □ ___

d) Place each of the following numbers in order of size – from greatest to least.

e) State the mean, mode and median for the following five numbers.

Mean:

Mode:

Median:

a) The owner of a local sports store has discounted every item in stock. Calculate the sale price for the following items.

	ITEM	RETAIL PRICE	DISCOUNT	SALE PRICE
i)	A baseball glove	$60	40%	
ii)	A bicycle	$640	20%	
iii)	A hockey stick	$135.95	12.5%	
iv)				

b) Round off the following numbers to the nearest tenth.

i)		ii)		iii)	

c) List the following rational numbers in order from least to greatest (may include fractions and decimals).

d) What fraction is halfway between _____ and _____?

Answer:

e) One number in the following set is not equivalent to the others. Determine which number it is and explain why.

Rounding, Ordering, Patterning, Fractions, Greater Than/Less Than

a) Round off the following numbers to the nearest hundredth.

i) | | ii) | | iii) | |

b) List the following integers in order from least to greatest.

c) What is the number 10 000 before:

d) By which number is the pattern decreasing?

_____, _____, _____

e) Reduce the following fractions to their simplest forms.

i) | | ii) | | iii) | |

f) Circle either < or > to indicate which number is larger in each of the following pairs.

i) | | < > | | ii) | | < > | | iii) | | < > | |

Place Value, Ordering

a) Solve the following.

i) ☐ × ☐ = ☐

ii) ☐ + ☐ = ☐

b) Write greater than (>), less than (<), or equal to (=) in the box between the two numbers.

i) ____ ☐ ____

ii) ____ ☐ ____

iii) ____ ☐ ____

c) Which number is modeled in the place-value chart below?

100 Thousands	10 Thousands	Thousands	Hundreds	Tens	Ones	Tenths	Hundredths	Thousandths

Answer: _____

d) Round each number to the nearest thousand.

i) ☐

ii) ☐

iii) ☐

e) Write the following group of numbers in order from least to greatest.

i)

Fractions, Percent

a) Record the following number in the accompanying place value chart.

Ten Thousands	Thousands	Hundreds	Tens	Ones	Tenths	Hundredths	Thousandths

b) Shade the model to show the correct fraction below.

Fraction =

c) Find the value of each percent.

i) _____ % of _____ = _____   ii) _____ % of _____ = _____

d) Place either a > or < symbol between the following pairs of fractions or decimals to indicate which is greater.

i) _____ ☐ _____   ii) _____ ☐ _____   iii) _____ ☐ _____

e) Convert the following improper fractions to mixed numbers.

i) _____ = _____   ii) _____ = _____   iii) _____ = _____

f) What is the correct way to write the number _____ in words?

Divisor, Dividend, Remainder

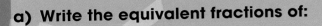

a) Write the equivalent fractions of:

i) _____ ⟶ _____   ii) _____ ⟶ _____   iii) _____ ⟶ _____

b) Calculate the mean, the median and the mode for the following:

	Mean =	
_____, _____, _____, _____, _____, _____, _____	Median =	
	Mode =	

c) Show each fraction as a percent.

i) _____ = _____ %   ii) _____ = _____ %   iii) _____ = _____ %

d) Divisor = _____, Dividend = _____, Remainder = _____.

What is the quotient? _____

e) What is the LCM of the following numbers. _____ , _____

f) Write the following number in expanded form.

[   ] =

_____